Sarah A Ramsdell

Spirit life of Theodore Parker

Through the Inspiration of Sarah A. Ramsdell

Sarah A Ramsdell

Spirit life of Theodore Parker
Through the Inspiration of Sarah A. Ramsdell

ISBN/EAN: 9783744744119

Printed in Europe, USA, Canada, Australia, Japan

Cover: Foto ©Thomas Meinert / pixelio.de

More available books at **www.hansebooks.com**

SPIRIT LIFE

OF

THEODORE PARKER.

THROUGH THE INSPIRATION OF

SARAH A. RAMSDELL.

BOSTON:

PRESS OF RAND, AVERY, & CO.

1876.

PREFACE.

THE circumstances and conditions under which this book was written render their brief narration important, in justice both to the medium and the inspiring intelligence.

It is due to the medium, a lady of unimpeachable integrity and candor, because, whatever judgment unbiased criticism may render upon the statements and sentiments herein contained, or their form of expression, as corroborative, or otherwise, of their purported authorship, it is quite certain that Miss Ramsdell can not, under the circumstances, be deemed to have originated them.

It is due to the invisible author, because the limitations imposed upon the utterance of his thoughts by the peculiarities of the medium's organization, and her limited literary culture, must necessarily have modified his effort.

Miss Sarah A. Ramsdell, the amanuensis of this volume, was, at the time of her development as a medium, engaged with her sister in the business of dressmaking at Lake City, Minn. Attending by invitation two or three spiritual circles, she found herself, at one of these gatherings, thrown into a semi-trance condition, and powerfully impelled to write the thoughts that crowded upon her mind.

This she did; and the result was, at several sittings, the production of short essays upon various subjects, purporting to be dictated by Theodore Parker in spirit-life.

Miss Ramsdell had *no acquaintance whatever* with the history, character, or writings of Mr. Parker. She had heard of him, in a general way, but had never had occasion to know or think of him particularly. Some of these essays were published in a spiritual journal, and others read before public assemblies in different places; being received with decided pleasure and appreciation. In the spring of 1869, the author announced his intention of writing a history of his spirit-life; but it was not commenced until the autumn of the same year.

When writing, the medium experiences great exaltation of feeling; a glow of intense pleasurable activity of the mental faculties, through which, thoughts and language seem to flow as from an inexhaustible fountain, without obstruction, save from the difficulty of writing fast enough to keep the stream of inspiration within the channel of language. Although intensely conscious of her occupation, she is so absorbed in it as to be practically unconscious of what is transpiring around her. The writing continues at each sitting so long as the mental control is retained by the spirit-author, and is resumed whenever a premonition of his desire to communicate is received.

Having enjoyed no other advantages of education than those afforded by a common school in the country twenty-five years ago, Miss Ramsdell has never been ambitious of literary distinction; nor had the thought of authorship ever crossed her mind. Finding herself thus unexpectedly selected for what she believes to be an important and beneficent work, she desires, in humility, to prove faithful to her spirit-guide; and therefore publishes this work at his desire. Having verified many of the facts communicated to her by the spirit, and feeling positive of his identity through the evidence interiorly imparted to her, she proposes still further to co-operate with him in these efforts to enlighten the world upon the great subject of man's spiritual nature and relations.

This work is one of a large and constantly-accumulating class of volumes purporting to be written or constructed in the spiritual world by authors who were once mortal inhabitants of the earth. Their intrinsic character alone will be the test by which the critical mind will judge of the probable truthfulness of these claims. It is not, however, at all incompatible with honesty and good faith on the part of the mediums, if the books thus written should not, in all cases, justify their claim of authorship.

The psychological border-land between the spheres of spiritual and mundane existence has not been yet so thoroughly explored as to enable any one in the body to dogmatize upon the conditions under which mortals and immortals may best meet and hold communion together. They who have passed from earth seem in our day and generation to be experimenting in this direction; and the crude results of their experiments, in the various forms of manifestation now so common, are properly the subject of patient study by those to whom they are submitted.

THE SPIRIT-LIFE OF THEODORE PARKER.

IN giving my spirit-life to the world, I have two points at issue. First I desire to show to the world my present existence, outside, untrammeled, and for ever from the flesh; show my whereabouts, condition, and occupation in my present locality. Now, in order to do this, I must get entire possession of my medium, through which my light will shine to the world. I must have her confidence, will, sight, and hearing; must let loose my cable, and draw her to the spirit-world; I must give her a tangible insight to my present sphere of use. This book contains my experience from 1854 until 1869, a period of fifteen years. I have been casting about for some time for the conditions by which I could labor to advantage. I now hope to give a work to the public that will be instructive, and worthy of a wide circulation.

The second point at issue is the development of the lady under my control, — a lady of great mediumistic worth, possessing rare powers in the background, to be brought forward when the demand calls for them.

Fraternally yours,

THEODORE PARKER.

[Given through the mediumship of Miss Sarah A. Ramsdell when in a semi-trance condition, 1869.]

CONTENTS.

10 CONTENTS.

THE SPIRIT-LIFE

OF

THEODORE PARKER.

CHAPTER I.

MY SPIRIT-HOME.

Home is a word we love to linger on ; it brings around our hearts a confiding trust and repose ; it is a word above all others most beautiful ; it touches the heart with new springs of action, lights up our saddest moments, and flings its halo of peace around the troubled waters of life. The word " home " thrills our whole emotional nature ; it gushes through our hearts like the rich cadence of some woodland bird, pouring forth its joy in song. My spirit-home,—it spreads around me like an ocean in repose, bathes me with the effulgent rays of a summer's noontide glory ; it fathoms my every wish and thought, finds me wherever in space the line of my research takes me ; it fills my whole being with delight, and wafts me on to higher realms of thought. My spirit-home ! ever fling your wealth of beauty around me, ever take me to your heart's deepest treasures of wealth and knowledge to the soul, ever bear me on the wings of love to fathom the mysterious courts hung out in

space, fling out thy starry petals of love to catch the
wayfaring children of earth, and bring them to a haven
of repose where earth's temptations can not affect the
soul. Thy gleaming lights are spread around my feet,
are hoisted high above my head, spread far and wide to
catch the onward march of mind. My spirit-home!
thy deep-seated attributes of truth and love I would
now speak. I would now hold my spirit-life out to the
world, to be tested by the hand of science, and fath-
omed by God's delving-rod of philosophical merit. I
would have the truth of my individualization now and
for evermore a settled fact on earth. For me to say
here, to declare through my present medium, that I still
possess the blessing of life, still possess every attribute
of mind, still possess the key-note to endless progression, is not enough for the world to-day. I must bring
forth evidence sufficient to substantiate my claim, I
must lay aside every barrier, and step back to the world
— Theodore Parker. When I cast off my worn-out
physical nature, I was under sunny skies, tended by
earth's ministering angels of love and mercy. Every
care that earth could give was freely bestowed; but
the law of Nature required her own, and I was forced
to give up my earthly tabernacle, forced to enter on a
new mission. I did not do that willingly, I felt I was
being defrauded; felt that the earth from which I was
being removed was full of mysteries that I had hoped to
fathom. I felt, that, deep within her receptacles, were
truths for me to reach. I did not suppose, from the
knowledge I then possessed, that the power would still
be left me. I supposed that my labors would tend to the
future; that earth would hold nothing in common for me:

that we were wide apart; that her storehouse of treasures would be closed against me; that far away in space
I should find my work. I felt confident there was no
power to chain my mind; but I desired a longer earth-
experience; desired a wider cope with theology; desired to bring Nature to combat, and show wherein theology had been weaving a web to get tangled in. I had
been reared, or rather I had reared a free platform
whereon I could stand, and wait for truths to come to
the rescue. I knew that error would surely be washed,
and I desired a life of materiality to help do the work.
I now thank my God that the wish was denied me, for,
in being removed from earth, I was brought nearer to
her. I find myself holding more knowledge of God's
laws than earth could have given me in the space of
time; I find myself invested with a power to unlock the
scientific world, which years of research on earth would
have only partially developed. I am brought nearer to
earth by my desire to fathom all the mysteries of cause
and effect, to uproot every hidden principle in her kingdom, to bring Nature to the platform for a thorough investigation into all her subtle chambers wherein God
has placed a key to unlock the passages that lead from
" nature up to nature's God." My soul drinks in the
beauties of earth with new delight, takes up her pages
of worth, and reads God's messages of love spread
broadcast and free. O thou God in nature! to thee
we look for truths to lead us up to thy throne eternal; to
thee we look for a basis-ground to rear our tabernacle
of trust and repose; to thee my soul goes back with its
divine afflatus of strength to leave no corner unsearched,
no background in thy broad arena unculled. I must

have thy treasured wealth, O earth! to lead me up the
steps of scientific exploration, — a field wherein all could
gather strength and courage for the battle of life.

CHAPTER II.

THE DUTIES OF SPIRIT-LIFE.

In the foregoing chapter, I alluded to my present
ability to visit earth, or, rather, to the fact that earth holds
me still by the power of social attraction and available
truths, that I must have in order to culminate a purpose which God has in store for me. My duty lies in
my ability, in my power to see and realize what is required of me. God gave me a mind of research, and
also gave me the power back of mind, the impetus of
will, to aid me in pulling down theories, and establishing
facts. Where God has given much, much is required.
My innate power of comprehension throws much responsibility around my soul. I am laboring to establish
a free platform, whereon every person can stand and
drink from the perennial spring of knowledge, unbiased
or untrammeled by creeds. My duties lead in that
direction. The sophistry of covering up truths and
promulgating error is time-worn and unprofitable; the
hungry mind is becoming fastidious. The sugar-coating
of egotism and self-delusion does not disguise the bitter
pill of partial destruction. The mind is no longer willing to be fed from that source of enjoyment. There

is a disposition to break in on a new field, where sympathetic emotion can be felt, and the brain not paralyzed for want of the proper digestive nutriment. I may be foolhardy to advance my system at the present time ; but " nothing venture, nothing have " is a true saying, and one I ever held to. My duty as a free-thinking, individualized character, surmounts every obstacle of policy, or any undue solicitude of public favor. Justice requires of me a full and descriptive detail of my present power to serve God and mammon ; or, in other words, to serve the kingdom of heaven by direct taxation on earth. I propose to divide my spirit-life into two cantos. The first shall embrace a portion of time while I was in the body, a wanderer on earth, with a spirit embodiment distinct in space. The second canto will take in my spiritual state, independent of my earth-form. A few years previous to my leaving earth (as the saying goes), I took up a new phase of life. I determined to live the religion I taught ; determined to embrace the Christ-principle in all the deeds done in the body ; determined to foster no ill-will to any one, to bind on my armor of trust and confidence in my own integrity of purpose to reach the standard to which I aimed. My spiritual existence was just as much a fact to me then as now. I knew the interior being was the true man ; I knew, as soon as dissolution of the body took place, I was winged for flight; I knew that the outstretch of worlds were within the pale of my research ; that eternity awaited me with its varied experiences that I must pass through ; and I determined to make my life one of duty, and reap my pleasures from that channel. Life always wore its serious face for me. I never could trifle

with time : it always seemed precious in my sight.
Earth held charms for me I can never forget; and,
while I sought in the flesh to advance every Christian
principle that came within my scope of experience, I
also sought a life to correspond with my teachings. Up
to 1854, my biographers would state my harassed condition of mind, and my unwavering determination to
push my theory through every obstacle that impeded
light to my famished soul. Creeds dropped away from
me very easily, because they were not consistent with
God's plan of salvation, which was to draw all nations
unto himself in the fullness of his own time. I could
not believe in a partial God that was so far removed
from justice and right that I was never crucified in that
direction. God ever rose above any impulse or change
in my estimate of his characteristics. He was the imperishable seed, rooted firm and deep in every thing
bearing life. The Bible version of God wraps him in
mystery. Now, if I am to have a Saviour outside of
any power of my own, I desire a full and complete
knowledge of that Saviour. Nothing short will satisfy
me, because I am so constituted, so organized, that mysteries contain no charm for me; and never can I worship a being clothed with attributes that do not reach
my soul. Up to the period last stated, the world looked
on me as an interloper; considered me averse to the
Christian religion, because I could not subscribe to
creeds; called me fanatic, a chosen one to mete out
destruction to a people who received religion second-
handed from God, and done up more to suit emergencies than as an appeal to reason, or as a guide to our
wandering footsteps. Thus, while the outside world

condemned me, I sought my convictions of right from nature, and my own innate purity of purpose.

The year 1854 found me a settled pastor over a peo-·ple living within the confines of Boston. I was chosen there to give light to a few that needed rest from theology. Their souls were famishing for the bread of life outside of the written testimony. Allegory was losing its power to succor the mind. Those few souls that needed me found me willing and ready to advance my theory of Unitarian salvation. I made my platform as broad as possible, and still it could not reach my wants. My hearers must have realized the dissatisfaction bearing down on me. I wanted to fly away from even that small restraint of creed. I wanted a worship that could take every soul to the altar of truth where no binding cord could lay its unction of claim.

CHAPTER III.

THE parish over which I presided could not accept my theory only half-way. The bare outlines held them while I was drinking from the fountain inexhaustible, and trying to purify the outward channels that moved society. My life found its pleasures in the sure knowledge I was gaining of the true religion. My labors were not thankless as far as the outward manifestations were displayed. I had many warm and genial friends, · who took my counsel and advice as something needed about their souls. They, no doubt, thought me wild

and radical after my outreach after principles that to
them seemed unnecessary to carry on a work of Christian duty; but the impetus that led me ever bore the
stamp of success. I do not know why it is; but my mind
wanders out on the chain of endless progression. I feel
that there is truth somewhere for every noble impulse
of my mind to grasp. I feel like taking earth on my
journey of research, and making her castles of error
disburse their flimsy stock of truth. I know my journey
leads up many a steep and rugged path; but my soul
puts on its armor of defiance, and I walk gladly on.
We too often let our souls lag for want of a purpose to
claim our attention, and start us forward to find our end
of God's progressive law. I never look back on my
earth-experience but to find fault with my gleanings.
Her pastures green should have fed me with more mo-
tive power for action. I was too inefficient in my own
strength. My energies should have been nursed by the
thunderbolt of Puritanic discord; I never should have
slumbered over a gulf of uncertainty; I should have
sought my shadowed future for seeds of truth to
have planted by the wayside, and made green every
field of labor wherein rested a doubt of ultimate success. But my friends in Boston and vicinity must
drink from the fountain of perpetual youth, made clear
and plain by the ovations of hope, presented by the
lagging energies of Theodore Parker. I shall culminate a purpose in your midst, that, fifteen years ago,
seemed likely to terminate in defeat. I shall hoist my
flag of truce, and come over to the enemy's quarters
with a diligence-express bearing the seeds of promise
that must root and grow in your midst.

CHAPTER IV.

It may be well to state my determination to push my theory in and about every triumphant seat of error in the land. I shall adopt the ways and means that I can best command. I shall send forth my speakers whenever I can harness them with my individuality, whenever I can control the synopsis of their fate without injury to any part of their being. This is a work that few in spirit-life undertake, because it is fraught with such uncertain results. There is no power to hold me back from duty. I must use my lever of strength to suit the demand of the times. I must lay my unction of hope on the altar of well doing, and abide by the results of my labors. I must grasp every tree that bears a branch of use to help carry on my work of destruction, to help lay aside the fettered yoke of ignorance and superstition. I would that my friends on the earth-plane could realize how much of my energetic hope is vested in their welfare, how much my spirit clings around the vesper-chimes of bygone days, how much I feel for the welfare of the world that gave me birth, how I cling to those old associations that bridge up the past with the present and future, how I long to break the spell, and let the captive world free to drink from the fountain that never runs dry! I must await the prestige of time, that ever deals gently and truly with the purposes of eternity. It may be remembered by my biographers, that, late in the fall of 1859, I was attacked with hemorrhage of the lungs; that it was considered advisable for me to flee to some warmer clime; that the terror of earth was bearing down on me with sure success. I witnessed the innovations of the destroyer with feelings that bordered on madness. I saw my sustaining props leaving me one by one, saw my inefficiency to keep my body before the public, saw the sure destruction of my earthly tabernacle; and I wavered in my idea of a just God. I started on my tour of investigation for ways and means to patch up the outward man, while the inner citadel of strength could pull away the obsolete theories that were traveling through the world without purpose or aim. I visited Santa Cruz, and found in her utmost limits of sunshine and shadow no spiral wreath of hope for me. The mystic touches of a funeral-pyre looked me in the face. I tried to think myself submissive; tried to see my way clear through the drifting events that were crowding around me; tried to think my duty lay in submission: but the calmness that was presented to the world was all on the fading surface. When I saw my physical power departing from me without regard to any skill of man, I formed a resolution to break away from the bonds of the Church. I thought, on entering on my untried mission, that I would have no binding cord but the one of friendship left on earth and in my heart. I had grown away from every restraint of church creed; I had no friendship for the tie; it hung around me like an error that my judgment disapproved of; it had its mountain-weight of infidelity to truth. I could not see my way clear while I had that attachment of inefficient aid; it bound me outwardly with its influence, while my mind was walking bold and upright away from the restraint. Let me here state, as an axiom of truth, that no individualized mind capable of ferreting out the ways and means to the true salvation should allow the stain of creed to mar the surface of the free torch presented to the world. I do not say there should be no systematic course in conducting Christianity on earth ; but I do say, let there be a broad basis of freedom underlying every institution that gathers the seeds of the Christian religion into its fold of worship. I do say, let Christ triumph, let his spirit enter every church-door with every individual entrance, and creed would soon drop from our midst, and we would find our way securely, supported by the props of love and duty to each other. The Christian religion was entered upon in the days when mind was in its infancy of attainment and research, when barbaric ignorance was creeping away from Christ's fold of love and mercy. The Christian religion has worked its way, step by step, into the soul-element of humanity ; has dug its way through every stage of development of mind and matter to the present time in the world's history ; and each offshoot from the old Mecca of intolerant despotism has taken a broader platform of liberal thought, and every outreach of principle has gathered more love into its stringent receptacles. The world has carried on her work with even-handed justice and mercy ; no serious outgushes of fanatic discord have disturbed the social elements of her quiet ways.

CHAPTER V.

The law of affinity has worked through every generation; the mind has affinitized with the element of success through every stage of harmonial design. The law of affinity has never been brought to bear on the conflicting elements that fashion the creed-bound world; all harmonious feeling has been disregarded; the mind has been coerced by dogmatic fancies; literal destruction, partial destruction, and God's sustaining grace, held forth for all to taste that willed, on the condition of church-security from the temptations of Satan, who was laboring to establish an institution that would run parallel with God's seat of glory. I often thought, while traveling my round of earthly duties, that the true and honest piety of heart was found in the by-ways of poverty. I have seen many a true soul struggling away from the Tempter, — struggling to maintain the outward respectability to harmonize with the interior integrity of purpose; and I say, " Of such is the kingdom of heaven." Such have wrought out their seat of honor by the self-sacrificing spirit of Christ; such are ready to enter on the holy mission of soul-redemption from the bondage of sin; and such are ready to lend a sustaining hand of help to those of weaker spiritual purposes in life. God's sustaining arm of progressive law hoists a flag of success for every individual. The meandering finger of Time works us through the earth-experience with vigilant dexterity, that notes every bar let down that lends a chance of egress to the enemy of

success. The last few years of my earth-experience
are fraught with sadness. My soul starts back on its
retrograde movement to patch up the deformities that
stand out apparent and bold, unprotected by earth's
sophistries; that cover up rather than eradicate the errors born in her vineyard. My ministerial career in
Boston binds me to that locality with unerring precision
of movement. I started to do a work there that the
hand of Time cut short. My friends tried their utmost
skill of purse, advice, counsel, and every free gift of
heart-and-mind dictation to keep me with them in form
while I promulgated the seeds their hungry souls thirsted
for. Their realms of thought were expanding under
the homœopathic doses of liberal food distilled from
nature and from humanity at large. They were not
contented to sit under their own vine and fig-tree as
long as it sprouted errors that reason held unprofitable.
I well remember hearing Rufus Choate expound the
science of religion. He was an able exponent in finan-
cial and political matters ; but Theology stood her ground
with him. His basis of salvation was the atoning blood
of Christ; but methinks, when Rufus Choate found himself winged for his spiritual platform, that the wide dif-
fusion of Christ's blood never entered into his compact
of salvation. The reason of my introducing Rufus
Choate here at this time and in this place is to expound a little on the ideas he put forth in the article
above mentioned. The great orator, gifted as few are
with eloquence that burned into the soul, left his lever
of strength unsheathed and folded away. Rufus Choate,
in spirit-realms, is searching deep and wide for the imperishable grains that he will drop on earth in due time.

The wily chief that darkens the doorway of faith must soon loose his dexterous skill : he has too long held the reins in governmental power, wherein the inner life of man is concerned. The science of religion, to the mind of Rufus Choate, appeared in tracing the bare outlines of man's historic career set forth in Holy Writ. Had he taken as deep a research in theology as he did in law, he would have culled his science from a broader field. Now, the science laid down in ancient history, and promulgated as the basis-ground for truth, has no more to do with the true religion — the religion of Christ's deeds of love — than it has in carrying us the overland route to California or Kamtschatka Isle, or any other remote region. It would seem more like a bar put up to impede our progress in the right channel. That book of saving grace is filled with scattered relics of pagan industry, compiled without regard to system, forethought, or knowledge ; and still it answers for a basis-ground of hope for the salvation of the whole human family, or the basis-ground of destruction for as many as do not subscribe to creeds.

CHAPTER VI.

SINCE I have been an inhabitant of the spirit-world, I have sought no discussive ground in a way that people fully understood my power and ability to deal with the errors of theology to an extent that earth never gave me. Now I propose to build up a fortress of

strength, and pick my way through every department
of theology. I propose to keep reason uppermost
in the chase after truth. I propose to discuss the
science of religion in a way, that every shade of basis-
ground will disappear from ancient history, and take
lodgement in the under-current of Christ's teachings.
When Herodotus pushed his vigilant war through the
Egyptian temples of hideous errors, he was only laying
waste the bulwarks that sustained the festering rubbish
of knight-errantry and the kingly power of ignorant
assumption. Herodotus, in bringing the Egyptians to
acknowledge his power, opened an avenue for the light
of Christianity. Lycurgus was another heathen ex-
plorer, that delved deep in fanaticism, picked his way
through the cruelties of an Egyptian court, and came
forth purified as a brand from the burning. Every
age has had its monument of strength in the heart
and purity of purpose in some individual, who puts
up the bar of progress at every stage of advancement
the world takes on. The old heathen philosophers
swept their boards clear of any stucco or varnish of
liberal sentiment. They believed in the holy wrath of
God's imperishable wisdom, manifested in his instruments of humanity. Heathen philosophers were averse
to any code of liberal teachings. Their intolerance and
ignorant superstition barred up all avenues from the
light of Christian duty manifested toward each other.
Their fire-gods and corrupt fetich of barbaric splendor,
served their coarse and uncultured minds. They supposed, in serving graven images likened to the Godhead, — whose superhuman skill at concealment they
could not fathom, — they were building a power on

earth that God would recognize with great pleasure. Barbarity, in any form, has no part in the Christian religion. It had its birth-hour when mind was steeped in the gross material of earth; when the soul was thought to take form in some planet, and the ruling spirit that assumed the greatest range of cruelty and power was expected to come forth from the second birth a representation of the higher constellations; and thus you see.the basis-ground for salvation to the heathen world was distinctive merit in cruelty. The starry pillar of truth was too far in the advance for their muddled vision to control. Lycurgus made way for the reign of Cæsar, the world-renowned conqueror, with the stamp of humanity underlying all his victories. The life of Cæsar is an illustrated boon of strength to the world; his fortitude, perseverance, and courage to maintain the supremacy of power, and foster in its midst the spirit of Christ. That increeping spirit of the loving Jesus has gathered new sprigs of worth to gladden the heart of every advance stage in knowledge. That is the basis-ground that has reared success, and the basis-ground that will maintain success throughout all time and eternity. Let me here enlarge upon that principle in humanity, because that is what will constitute our heaven, whether on the earth-plane, or when earth shall have yielded up the true man to the infinite seat of progress. What is there in the whole life of Jesus but love, manifested through every channel wherein he had a purpose to aid humanity? He never stopped for motives. The fervid outgushes of love ever impelled his movements; his words of chastisement were ever given with a basis of love to further their import. Both Jew and Gentile were served alike from his storehouse of love. He spread his table alike for all that came within his knowledge of research. It was no flimsy coating to disguise a bitter pill, but a free gift from a heart overflowing with kindness. His self-abnegating spirit made success over temptation an easy matter. The power of the destroying angel had no charms for him. He was incased in the armor of holy purposes. He meant his life should be an example to the world in which he lived. He inherited his meek and loving spirit from his mother Mary, and his intrepid daring from his father Joseph. His power to perform miracles was his mediumistic worth. Spirits ever found him accessible. He was so imbued with the attributes of the higher life, that his guardian spirits impressed his whole being with his holy mission to humanity. He lived in the two worlds. Death had no victory over him. The higher life was his home, and death the doorway through which he must pass. That knowledge, taken to the heart and soul as Jesus took it in, would bless humanity with divine purposes to each other. We are not so unlike Jesus as we suppose. We have the crustations of selfishness to contend with which Jesus did not possess ; and we have the illiberal sentiments of ghastly theology that dares to pick places in the vast storehouse of eternity, where some must wrestle with destruction, and cry out for the God of Israel to have compassion on their souls, with no answering response from a God who immolates his Son on the shrine of affection for humanity. Jesus had no such theology to contend with. His disciples and followers were ignorant of creeds. If Jesus was the true Messiah, they were all willing to ac-

cept him ; were willing to give up their burnt-offerings
and sacrificial altars, and accept Christ as their light. All
they asked was assurance of his genuineness to serve
them.   They had no bottled-up portions of excellence
that clamored for upper seats in God's kingdom, with
egotistical assurance of superior merit.   Those olden
times had the merit of simplicity of heart.   What they
lacked in culture and refinement they showed forth in
courage and zeal to maintain some fortress of strength
for future use.

CHAPTER VII.

In the crucifixion of Christ, there is a great deal of
allegorical matter, — a great deal of the spurious mixed
with the true.   His advent into life was no miraculous
interposition of Providence ; it was merely the process
of natural law, through which he became manifest to the
world : and his exit from earth followed on his failing to
meet the demand of the ignorant classes that he had to
deal with.   His ascension was no physical flight, but a
soul-redemption from sin, but portrayed in the figurative
language of flesh and blood.   It does seem as though
the nineteenth century should be above the supposition
of crude materiality entering the precincts of heaven.
There is no law to sustain matter above the confines of
earth.   Christ died, was buried ; and his redeemed spirit
went on its mission to fathom the world that was already
familiar to him by his pure and unassuming earth-life.
Christ's element of success was recognized more after

his departure from earth. That spirit of meek forbearance troubled the hearts of his disciples: they began to realize his worth, and miss the charm of his presence; and would, no doubt, have recalled him, could such have been. But the death of Christ at that time was auspicious for the world's improvement: his holy spirit surmounts every difficulty that bars the road to progress. Christ is the illuminated page that will ever be read to advantage. The history of Christ is the history of a redeemed spirit on earth, — the history of all pure and holy purposes embodied in earth-form. As an example of purity, power, and self-abnegation, Christ has never been excelled; and, though ages may roll along the track of time, there may not be another such combination of holy assurance given to humanity. There is a spell around his name that will ever lend its influence around society. Let Christ be man or angel, it matters not: he has been the sustaining strength in every reform since Calvary reared her ebon cross to stain the character of her written testimony. The Jewish nation labored to establish a broader basis of salvation for the human family. Christ seemed inefficient to them as a Saviour and Redeemer: they sought an embodiment of external power. They could not appreciate the indwelling Spirit of saving grace: the external world was all they could fathom to secure support to their upward career of worldly achievements. Power to them was distinctive glory in heaven; and, as Christ assumed no wordly distinction or honors, they thought him an interloper, not capable of serving them: therefore they sought and obtained his overthrow. And, to this day, the Jewish nation remains unreconciled to any plan of sal-

vation : they are wanderers on the face of the earth,
seeking the divine afflatus still, but with something of
the old stoicism, that power rules in the kingdom of
heaven. The Jews have fought dry their well-springs
of success ; their shattered glory is the Rubicon of error
over which they have passed. The Jews are merging
toward extinction ; their holocaust of strength is nearly
expended ; there is no harmonious element to keep
peace in their souls ; the dewdrops of the harmonial
law has never entered their inner lives. The Jewish
nation will one day become but a ripple on the great
ocean of time, and eternity will have caught the waif-
lings to the utter disregard of human will or power.
Eternity lays its fangs of strength on all of earth's possessions, from the tiniest flower to the wide range of
upheaved mountain skill. All Nature has its part in
the resurrection morn of ethereal grandeur and systematic beauty; all Nature drinks from the fountain of the
unseen ; her spiral points pierce the elements of success
to sustain her unwearied efforts at perfection. Nature
goes on in successive routine : it fashions and builds for
God's storehouse of eternity.

CHAPTER VIII.

THE widest range of thought is sure to quench its
thirst at every passing stream ; gathering new forces and
beauty for its detail of encounters from one stage of life
to another. Man little realizes on earth the power given

the mind for expansion : it doubles its growth at every sweep in the great ocean of eternity. Were I to say here the mind of man possesses the innate seeds, or, in other words, the culminating particles, to rear a world, I should no doubt be deemed insane ; but, nevertheless, the hand of science will yet demonstrate the fact to the world. I ask, what has reared the world to-day from chaotic sameness to its present point of interest and beauty, but the mind of man ? But some will say, man has only brought out and fashioned what was in the beginning. Allowing that to be so, allowing the world to be a crucible where man is experimenting, does it not show conclusively that mind will never stop picking in matter until her every receptacle that contains a seed to sprout and grow is laid open for investigation ? And who shall say mind can not create when it understands the process of creation ? There is no cheat in God's law of development : it is systematic process from beginning to end. There are no lost keys to any drawer of the material universe, and each mind can and will unlock its own particular drawer. It is not always easy or best to unlock the future before time, or promulgate undue circumstances ; but I must throw out this fact here, that time will clothe with truth, that, in less than a century of time, the mind of man will cope with the external forces to create a world. It is no more than mind in eternity, or mind disembodied from matter, is capable of doing at the present time. My life-history will reveal facts instead of fables. It will be no revelation clothed in mystery for mind to wander around, and become fogged in its attempts to extricate a few grains of truth that reason will find, however deep the rubbish. At the present day, spirit-communion is no concealed fact. It is an ushering-in of the New Jerusalem; the time earnestly looked for in every generation; the glad tidings of great joy come to bless the world in its spring-time of social and moral elevation. It sprouted in the midst of refinement and wealth; and it will accumulate strength to maintain its support, until every locality in the universe of matter is sprinkled with its divine afflatus of truth and love.

CHAPTER IX.

THE more I attempt to harness on my earth-life, the more barrenness I discover in fields that should have grown ripe to my advantage; and, but for that old theological atmosphere of oppression, I would be wandering in fields where now I only catch the shadowed light. I will refer to my spiritual growth from 1854 to 1859, shadowed as it was by the conflicting elements of time. 1854 found me verging toward a social reform; or, in other words, seeking to instill the need of rendering the social element into the folds of the Christian Church. It was like a galvanic battery to the lunatics in an insane asylum. It touched every fiber of the world's holy horror of mixing up any thing with religion but burnt-offerings in the shape of special prayer-meetings, special days of worship, and special demagogues or prelates to keep sacred their fold of contracted sentiment and pent-up selfishness. Those days to me were fraught with bitterness of spirit. I could not brook the many insults offered me, without sinking some of the wormwood and gall into my own secret caverns of thought. I well remember the anathemas raised against me; well remember the sounding clarion of public animosity and hatred that warbled forth its discordant notes throughout my field of action. I could not labor to advantage in the frozen atmosphere of undulating sentiment. It paralyzed the life-blood of hope, and chilled the impetuosity of my movements toward sustaining my platform of truth toward humanity. Were I to step back, clothed with the habiliments of earth, or to step back to that point in my life where I wrestled with uncertainty in regard to the soul's ultimate success over time and eternity, I could meet the exigencies of doubt from ten thousand worlds, and find myself buoyant in maintaining the platform I started on in 1854. The past can never be bridged over nor walled up: it will ever remain a thread in the great web of life, a reference-mark, keeping our time and place in eternity. My past life is one of the distinctive elements that holds me to the present and future. You can no more get away from the past than you can from the future: they are the two diverging lines in life, — the one impelling us forward, the other holding our march by the law of recompense that never fails in its duty toward the children of earth. In starting on a tour of investigation, we should have our lamps trimmed and burning. We should delve as far into the future as we can with benefit to our reason; and, in fact, we can not sink logic deeper than reason will hold true. Our reason is our safeguard, our monitor of strength, our impelling force to action. Therefore, when we would have facts instead of fables, let reason hold the light to guide the way to knowledge. My early years of earth-experience were fool-hardy with expectations of a successful career through life. That was before I had weighed the public mind by any scales but hope. Youth is ever imaginative, ever building airy castles to crumble at the breath of public disfavor. My life was even-handed as far as I could make it by steady application to study, and a determination to overcome the prejudice and fanatic discord which came within the scope of my experience. My whole earth-career was simply a trial adventure, — a breaker put forth to battle with the storms and quicksands on the rolling sea of life. That I did not fill my measure to completeness in earth's diluted beverages of wisdom is now fully apparent to me; and, if that sentence can have any weight to the gleaners in earth's vineyards, it will not have been uttered in vain. When people start out on a platform to evangelize society, they will ever find themselves rowing against the current; will find life spicy and full of acrimony; find themselves a disturbing element in the slough-pools of indolent ease, and warring with the spirit of rest to the world's discomfort, and to the world's dread of being found wanting in the essential elements to success. I do not regret my earth-experiences: they were all needed for my purposes of action; all held out their hand of help to aid in the great battle of life. Through trials and tribulations, the soul radiates to glory, and also radiates to the true worth in humanity. I have friends in Boston and vicinity that I visit daily: the cord of love and friendship has never been severed; its binding influence cheers my onward march. Boston is the acme of earth's soluble friendships: it reared my Christian growth, and supported my lagging energies when public disfavor trampled me with its heel of vengeance. There are many hearts in Boston that throw out their silver linings for me to catch the reflected purity of their souls. In wafting my thoughts backward, I seem to catch the welcome glance of friendship, and the proffered hand of love; I seem to hear the whispered farewell at my departure for the sunny isle that gave me rest from suffering beneath her cool and sunny skies. When I take up my backward track, there is ever an impetus to cheer the local habitations of earth's children with the effulgent rays of spirit-communion. I can not rest me quiet in my spirit-home. I must seek to dispel illusory customs of earth; seek an entrance into the fields of theology, and brave again the contumacious doubting of the world. My seed-time and harvest is not completed on earth; I have only set my stakes, and measured out my ground for the present, and am awaiting the weather-sweep of time to make favorable the conditions for sprouting the seeds which I shall promulgate on earth. When Herodotus warred in the Egyptian temples of fame, he spilled the Carthaginian blood of ancestral bigotry and fanaticism. He warred with precepts and principles; he warred with the illiberal sentiments of ghastly theology; he warred with the hideous daring of Grecian autocrats, who shuffled all responsibility into the church militant, which was the cesspool through which all found a passage leading to life eternal. Since Herodotus'

reign, the camp-fires of a more liberal sentiment have
lighted up every period in the cycle of time.   Herodotus was a Grecian king, a stipulator for the am-
nesty of power through the channel of the operative
law of social reformation.   Every age has had its by-
play to foster the element of progress ; every age has
suited the action to the word of renovation ; every move
has been forward march in the line of battalion array.
The pickets on duty have warned us of every approach
on the enemy's quarters.   And those guards on duty
clearly discover the lion at bay by the howling demand
of the successful monster that ever tramples what it
means to destroy.   Let me again refer to the science
of religion.   Let me take up the life-history of religion,
its time, place, and culture, its advent into the world,
and its exit therefrom, without a thread left in the old
loom of ancient mythology.   Religion is based on God's
law of harmony : its fundamental precepts are love,
hope, and trust ; its organized institutions should be an
even-handed justice spread broadcast throughout humanity, and a friendship made soluble by deeds done in
times of need.   Earth should hold no religion, only
what comports with the highest attributes of man's
instinctive nature.   All other is froth on the surface of
human wants ; all other is a needless expenditure of
time and money, as far as fostering the true seeds
of worship are concerned ; and all other is the harbinger of the coming wind, that will sweep the chaff from
its seat of honor.   The science of religion is the master-
key that will unlock the fountain that has too long been
choked by the accumulated rubbish of all ages of time;

and the clear and purling stream of silvery love and friendship will flow from the old despotic fountain of selfish inharmony and strife.

CHAPTER X.

RELIGION is a want to the human mind; it is a necessity to the soul, a peace-offering from God to man; it is a sentiment that needs the fostering hand of love to keep green. Religion sprang up in the dark ages, when the soul craved food to sustain its highest functions of being; when no power but God's, speaking through the essential element of humanity, could stay around the benighted hearthstone of darkened mythology. God speaking in his thunderbolts of terror was losing its charm. There was a congenial softening of heart growing out of the long-continued rasping and warfare: it flooded its own spirit, and gave birth to a new type of questionable religion, or questionable theology, because religion and theology are two distinctive elements in society, — the one harnesses up a team for show, the other picks its way on foot, if need be, but still intent on finding out the needs of humanity. Religion is an undercurrent that moves along with the tide of fashion; and when fashion sickens, as is ofttimes the case, religion holds out her panacea of strength to grasp the sickened soul into her haven of rest. Religion is the fundamental earthquake that will upheave and demolish every type of spurious metal the world takes on as a harness of salvation. The advent of the Christian religion, or what is termed the Christian era, is a marked period in the world's history : it fashioned its growth after the hidden teachings of Christ ; it has run parallel with ancient history since ancient history assumed the power to save mankind. Religion has a sway entirely its own ; it never builds from any particular style ; its principles of structure are firmly rooted, branching ever in the direction of use ; taking up life as best it may, still intent in serving for the highest good, aiming always to ·upplant evil by sowing the good seed of loving-kindness that will root where illiberal dealings can find no entrance. Religion strips herself clear of any outward show or manifestation of egotism ; she never takes more than her due of credit for favors bestowed ; she asks no high tariff of the world's applause ; she simply asks the privilege of showing her skill at renovation, at tearing down pillars of show, and erecting structures of strength to meet the demand of human wants. Religion is a true financier, delving in the cesspools of political warfare, and toning up the moral functions of the parties in power. Religion is destined to sweep the board of public welfare of all the rubbish of false pretense and all false stars that shine to no purpose in life. Religious culture is the ebb and flow of the tidal waves of current events that fashion the world we live in ; religious culture would string our lives with pearls did we but let go of self long enough to grasp the true essence of her mission. She can not feed us with the true light of revelation until we open our hearts to receive the light from her many-hued tapers that are spread broadcast and free. There is no tax to be paid on our gleanings in religious culture; we can take all we can digest without fear of its hurting our digestive functions. It is a harmless remedy for all the ills of life; it clears our pathway of all false rubbish, of all graven images, sprouted for no use to the soul's salvation, but a lumbering car filled with weapons of destruction to slay our peace and comfort. Religion grasps our true life; it sprouts no other for us to cling to; it radiates around no false precepts or examples; it tunes its harp for the great choir of humanity. Religion has set its seal of contempt on all false doctrines that soothe us to slumber over an abyss of doubt and uncertainty. No false coloring suits the majestic grandeur of her quiet ways; she feels no impulse for a life of double dealing; she sips the nectar of truth from God's vast arena of nature, and fills every heart that is open to receive the free and proffered gift.

CHAPTER XI.

NOTHING can so suit the heart of humanity, nothing can so delve around all selfishness, nothing so pick its way to the spirit of unrest, as the true and shining light of religion. It garners its stores with always a door left open for the wayfarer who is being pelted by the storms of adversity. Christ was a religious man from intuition. His spirit sought the wants of human nature; he affinitized with the highest element in humanity; he ever sought the world's vortex of confiding trust, in the highest means to serve the greatest good. Christ left his spirit of religion to bless the world; he

left his footprints of princely daring and virtues to guide
the stranded ones of earth to their haven of safety. There
never has been a light in the world that has shone so
radiantly, lighting up all the by-ways, sending its halo
of glory into all desolate places, and weaving its web of
royal brightness to hang over the earth in her times
of moral darkness. The religion of Christ was heart-
felt, and realized as his sustaining strength when earth
threw her mantle of trouble around him. Religion, in
the abstract, signifies harmony of soul with the divinity
of purpose; but the world has mixed the true purpose
of religion with the outward show of mock ceremony,
until one-half of the minds on earth to-day never dip
deeper than the customs of past generations for succor
to maintain the soul. What but the light of revelation
from God's storehouse of intuitive reasoning could grasp
this unseen lever of strength, and apply it for the
world's improvement! God shines forth his luminations
of truth in every corner of the world's use. The
gradual unfoldment of divine purpose creates no jar in
the infinitude of mind and matter. The even hand of
a beneficent Creator smooths all the rugged places by
some straying ray of truth let loose for the occasion. Divinity shapes our course most unflinchingly. It is no ner-
vous hand that grasps the rudder of our destiny; it is
no tremulous wave on the great ocean of eternity that
moves our course of action. We were not dropped here
without a purpose to culminate, without the power
given us to locate our destiny, without the pickax of
accumulation left within our grasp. God's law of recompense never cheats us a particle, never sifts an error
in our path but what Reason could pick to pieces if she

willed to do so. But when we allow reason to lay dormant, and let out the job of thought to the highest bidder after wordly renown, why call God a cheat, and say he has harnessed our team, but left us no driver, when it is plainly evident he intends us to be our own teamsters along the road of life ? And he has so fashioned our team, that it has the capacity for expansion or contraction ; the capacity for gaining strength by accumulation, or becoming weakened by disease. God ever stares us in the face with our mission ; ever puts up bars for us to climb over : and, if we fall in the attempt to master the difficulties in our pathway, the right hand of fellowship is extended from the spiritual platform to keep good our efforts at success.

CHAPTER XII.

THE harmonial law is working in unison with the law of religious culture. There is sympathetic emotion between the two elements of reform ; they are starting out on a tour of investigation, with the determination to assist each other in overcoming the difficulties of priestly triumph. The harmonial law is destined to become the law of success. It has picked its way through numberless difficulties, and still stems the current of public disfavor. When the dynasties of Europe sought the overthrow of Charles the Second, it was in accordance with the primeval teachings of the ancestral line of successive generations, that no power but kingly power, manifested in the gibbet, in racks of torture, and in the guillotine, or scaffold of impious sacrifice, should claim a seat at their national board of honor; and hence the harmonious outreach of principle at that period was allowed no footing. But subsequent years have fostered the germ that sprouted when earth could not contain its growth. The Babylonish captivity was a more ancient onslaught on the principle of harmonial growth. The world was flooded to secure that harmony that after-years sought to overthrow. The Babylonish captivity served as food to maintain the fierce and cruel system through which the world was then passing; and yet, in this nineteenth century of moral and intellectual growth, there is no work from the pen of any inspired writer, that can push its way up to the hearthstone of every nation as that time-worn book of fabled mythology and sanctified cruelty. The Bible, proclaimed as the word of God from every pulpit in the world, bearing the stamp of legalized Christianity, abounds in atrocities that this age can not enact, even in imagination, without a shudder and a creeping-away of soul from the pictured scenes of ancient history, legalized to the world as God's token of mercy and love. I wonder at the fashion of keeping food that does not serve our purpose; of passing round a dish that all partake of, but few like or relish: but I find, from my spiritual locality, that earth is creeping away from the trap set so many years ago, and sprung at every footfall of progress, until its springs are becoming old and rusty from decay. I hold no reverence for a system of laws that can not withstand the picking hand of Time, and remain firm in the united effort at success. I hold no reverence for

a theologian who climbs the hill of science, and sprouts
no new themes for the distilling dews of admixture
to lift from the rubbish of the past. I hold no truth
sacred, or beyond cavil, that flinches at the hand of investigation. The Old World garners her stores of
wealth in accordance with her valuation of monopolized
grandeur and kingly assumption. . The Old World is
beating her bars of iron will against any invasion of
democratic power. The master-spirit of ancient chiv-
alry finds no response from their fattened cloisters of
papal glory. England masters every emotion of sympathetic daring brought to her knowledge; she allows
no straying sheep from her fold of domineering greatness; she folds her hands with the utmost complacency
over her systems of oppression. The serfs that flood
her streets are a libel on her escutcheon of power; she
has never entered into compact with the spirit of Christ;
the herald of mercy has never entered her door of
oppression, that is closed to every call but the one
of moneyed interest. When England drives a more
liberal team in this great world of cause and effect, she
will feel the ennobling influences that wrought out freedom on the American continent. The world is filled
with oppressive systems; and the Anglo-Saxon blood is
the master-key that binds the cord of stringent measures
around society. The Anglo-Saxon fibers that constitute the underpinning of American society are sprouting
their helmet of strength into every channel of arbitra-
tion in this great world of commerce and strife. There
is no reason why America should not pick her way into
every department of human zeal and courage. America
should foster no feeling of supremacy, but should set

to work with a movement of soul to galvanize the
heathen world with the aroma of knowledge and freedom.   The advantage America claims over all other
countries is due to her liberal platform of deal; is ow-
ing to her free passports of strength, that slumber a
dead weight on all other nationalities in the world.
While I maintained my earthly tabernacle, I fought
every system of oppression, I warred with every monster that reared a head above the confines of public
good.   I have never changed one iota in my sentiments
with regard to the demon of oppression in any form.   I
still hold to a legalized surrender of every perch that
collects the fauna of society, whether that perch be hid
from public view, or flaunted forth in genteel society.

CHAPTER XIII.

WHEN the great war proclaims the world's salvation
from the law of ignorance, then will the evils that now
surround mankind drop apart, and light will shine
through the darkened temples of defamation.   There is
nothing that so hampers the mind as distrust.   It is like
a darkened veil thrown before our outward vision, im-
peding our progress, and making us stumblers on the
highway of life.   It is a true saying, that "life is a
thorny road to travel;" and many a bramble and thorn
will spring up in our path unless we cultivate the soil
as we proceed on our journey.   Life is one long illustrated roadway; and the illustrations are pictures in

allegory, descriptive of our inner struggles around temptations that beset our pathway. Earth is man's trial course of action. We may beat our prison-doors ever so much; but, until the hand of Fate springs the lock, we are prisoners on the course of time; anglers around the great bait of eternity, throwing our hook into ten thousand pools, to find it nibbled by some speculator on ·our field of action. There is nothing so worthy of investigation as God's plan of salvation. It should claim the attention of every sane mind on earth; it should be brought to the door of every child's understanding, there to await the light of reason to lay aside every barrier of restraint. The world has too long sought safety from destruction in her Hellenic authors of doubtful report. She should have a cataplasm or antidote of a soothing nature after this purging process of fire and brimstone that has lit the target hurled at so many generations, and never swept the board of any of the evils it sought to destroy. I must say here and now that I pity any mind bound to any theology extant in the world, with no loophole of egress to confront the enemy of progress. The Sicilian captive, bound with the fettering chains of anarchy, was no more a captive than the stickler to one code of worship, one code of laws, and one code of morals, for this age of reasonable outgrowth from dogmatic prejudice and assumption. What Hecletus saw on the Tower of Babel puzzled the Greek philosopher. He wondered at the idiosyncrasies of benighted Babylon; he wondered at the deformities of heathen barbarity. As system after system sweeps along the course of time, the liberal hand of justice points the way to the sunny side of life. Thermopylæ

was destroyed to suit the exigencies of power. The Old
World is filled with its sacrificial altars, its crisp and dry
rubbish, that makes the Past seem like old age creeping
along in its dotage to overtake the gay and happy child,
who springs at the touch of the myriads of keys that
unlock its bright and buoyant soul. The Past is the
stagnant water in the great pool of life, and no drainage
from the nineteenth century can bring so much as a ·
silver ripple across its sullen face. Its shores will beat
against the Future like a brand of despair hurled at the
retreating enemy in advance. The mushroom type of
society ignore present and future revelation ; they accept the Bible as a moiety to sustain the even hand of
Justice, that never flinches in doing an act of duty. Let
our acquirements be what they will in the seeds of old ́
theology, Justice never tampers with the affairs of men.
She clothes herself with the habiliments of truth and
equity, and warbles forth no strains of discord. Our
pillar of strength is our fortitude to branch out in life,
and hold on to the rein of just deal with our fellow-
beings. I no longer marvel at inconsistencies in human
nature. Every individual possesses the distinctive element to rear a platform of free purposes of action ; but
there is always a hinge loose that makes the platform
shaky, and beyond our control to manage to advantage.
The next course pursued is, instead of seeking a remedy
to remove the defect, we give up the ship entirely, and
sink to the float-bridge, that is ever ready to catch the
unstable and dilatory ones of earth. Human nature
lays no plan of escape from the vestments of sin. Sin
binds itself, with its armor of truth, to the purpose it
serves. There is no sin but what has its concordant

element of defeat growing beside the still waters of despair. The word "sin" implies the absence of good; sin Anglicized implies inharmony in the constituents moving our course of life. Now, the absence of the element which we all condemn, and which we all imbibe, would leave the world in a state of nude purpose. The element of conflict is as necessary as the element of peace. Both rest quiescent in their orbit of perpetual movement. The gyrating hand of Time can never pick the system of good and evil apart. They are twins in the field of cause and effect; they are co-workers for the kingdom of heaven; Siamese in nature and principle to maintain the binding cord of unity of purpose to serve mankind. Sin has no separate purpose from good. It bears its relative value in the current articles before the world. Sin never yet mastered the emotion of good. Good is more tranquil in nature than the opposing element, leading us to suppose the ascendency has been gained over the more quiet movements of the soul. After Nature has had her fits of howling discord, the golden-crowned monarch lifts his head exultingly, and proclaims the sure defeat over assumptive power. We, in our nature, partake of the great solar systems that encompass our being. The laws that govern our natural orbit on earth run parallel with the laws that govern the universe of matter. Mind is the deific figure, the stamp-mark branded on our ultimate possessions over gross materiality.

CHAPTER XIV.

THE solar systems govern the harmonial law of our interior individualization. The solar key unlocks the prisoned earth, and lets her captives free. The solar nucleus springs our system of nerve-power, unhinges our slothful habits, and awakens us to the grandeur of activity. We are a part and parcel of the great machinery of natural laws, acted upon by every thing in the kingdom of Nature; acted upon by every ray of light from the great mining-house of God; prone to do evil because it is a concomitant in Nature; prone to do good because that balances the wheel of error. Has not every person having a foothold on earth had to acknowledge the ever recurring presence of the smitten angel, that passed from the house of God with visor drawn, and the brand of dishonor hurled at his retreating figure? The Devil, it would seem, has occupied every seat of honor; he has had his reign supreme on earth, and broke bread with the angels in Heaven; and, to this day he rules the affairs of men with systematic precision of movement, coupled with a determination to revenge the insult shown him at the gate of heaven. The Devil rules by force of circumstances: he picks his way with perfect adaptation to the call received and the means to overcome to obey the call. The Devil seldom asks charity: that spirit of meekness does not suit his dignity of purpose. I ever found in my earth-experience that the temptations of Satan ever followed on our letting down the bars at our vineyard of strength, and leaving no watch at the gap. The Devil is perfectly fool-hardy; fear never enters the vocabulary of his speech; he trails the flag of truce in the dust, and beats no retreat as long as the word " conquer " stares him in the distance : and another peculiarity his Majesty assumes is his deft and cunning ways, ofttimes leading us with his hand of skill, that assures us of perfect safety, when it is shaking with the palsied effort to maintain the disguise until we are anchored on the side of unsafe footing. The Devil masters every emotion of guile, spreading his wings with perfect *sang froid;* clasping you by the hand, and showing his face of honest integrity, but with a sly wink that bodes mischief in the future. And so on I might trace the subtle winding of King Evil to obtain a lasting footing with the children of earth; but as that is not my speciality in this present work, although, at some future time, I may show the monstrous bugbear, bearing the term Devil, to the world, holding a part in all materiality and in all spirituality, showing him to the world as a necessary evil, branded with contempt, but bearing the stamp of use.

CHAPTER XV.

THERE is one point to be gained over society before the harmonious element can sweep the world's board of error; and that one point is as defiant as the unsheathed weapon of a daring foe. This braggadocio of defensive skill is world-renowned for its activity in picking

4

seeds of use from the dry and barren fields of theologic
lore.　There are, no doubt, morsels of worth interlaced in
that mighty fabric composed to suit the emergencies of
the heathen world.　It never was designed or labeled
food for all time : if such had been the case, why has
the stamp of discontent found its way to the sideboard
of every generation ?　why have there been anglers
after truth not found in sacred history ?　why have our
palates refused to discover the secret aroma that has its
binding worth above any tinsel or glitter of false presentation ?　The Bible is filled with its seeds of corrup-
tion; its fields of bloody umpire, that the soul revolts
and creeps away from.　I ask of any mind to-day, lighted
by the torch of reason, how the Bible version of the
world's formation accords with their faculty of thought ?
No sane mind at this age considers the miraculous conception of the world's birth, promulgated in history, as
an appeal to their credit, unless the statement can be
dressed in some figurative style to suit the demand of
reason.　Man's reason is his highest orbit of sense, his
highest faculty of intuition, the lens through which he
looks to detect the spurious from the true : reason is
not soluble by any scales but the preponderating law
of cause and effect.　The world is fast losing its starting-point.　It is no longer assumed by learned minds
that it sprang from chaotic ruin, or that it took form in
the space of one week, and rolled out into ethereality
ready for the redeeming hand of man, not yet fashioned.　I wonder at the inconsistency of thought.　I wonder at the strange idiosyncrasies in human nature as
applied to the religious element fostered in society.　I
wonder at man's faith to obtain succor from dry husks,

potted down, and seasoned with the bitter herb of mal-
ice prepense. It is a sad thought that human nature
possessed the attribute to derive pleasure, hope, or sympathetic emotion, from the presentation of mock heroism,
and selfish anarchy, protruded at an age when Devils
were manufactured in heaven. Why is it that people go back for messages from God? Why not receive
them daily, and bind them as a truth about their hearts?
Why pick in fields that have been culled so long, to the
exclusion of receiving fruit ready to be dropped by the
angelic band traveling for the world's restoration to
happiness and content?

CHAPTER XVI.

MAN fashions his own life; that is, he binds the
nectar of peace about his heart-strings, or fills his field
with patches of barren waste. Youth should be early
taught the financiering of life; should early take up the
lesson of self-culture; should early promise a gift to the
soul, and scorn to break the promise. Earth is filled
with starry gems that the recording angel is toiling to
pick for his crown. The hope that is vested in uncertainty has the pinched-up expression of despair. Let
the light of a just knowledge expand the well-springs of
action, let mankind fill their storehouses with the good
seed that ripens to advantage, and soon the world will
be rid of the half-formed fruit that now appeals at the
doorway of heaven. I have before remarked, that
God's laws were a systematic course of activity, work-

ing round the great central sun of their orbit; and why
should man show a less systematic course? why should
not each circle in his orbit of motion count as a benefit
in the great stream of life? Man needs to be awakened
to the great responsibility of his mission in life; he
needs to be galvanized with the lightning-flashes from
the great distillery-house of truth; he needs to have
the lighted taper of damnation hurled at the retreating
figure of Sin: and its echoing wail will be an anthem of
joy to the world. I have nearly completed the first
canto of my spiritual state of existence. I have given
it as a prelude, or connecting link, in the chain of my
drifting life; I have handed it back to the world simply
as a stepping-stone to reach my present locality; I have
made this treaty of peace as connected as the circumstances and conditions through which I have labored
would permit of: it is simply grains of earth-culture
given from a spiritual platform, and tied with a string of
truth. I must touch one more point of my earth-career;
must pick up my staff of infirmity, and taste again the
bitter cup presented by the hand of love. My last
earthly journey was fraught with great inharmony of
spirit. I was leaving my native shores; was leaving
my dear and time-tried friends; was leaving the associations of my whole ministerial career, entering upon a
new field of adventure, with no strength of nerve or will
to struggle in untried paths. My spirit beat its prisoned
walls for freedom to lift the clouds that hung over my
future. I knew that my friends were being entirely
shut out from my future on earth; I knew the destroying angel was following in my wake, ready to lift me
overboard when Earth had duly performed her mission.

The angel of death is seldom met with pleasure. We can view his shadow in the distance, and feel no thrill at the danger he represents; but when we see the enemy on our track, with no hope of re-enforcements, the battle-ground of life presents a sad and troubled scene. There is nothing in my whole earth-experience that so touches my memory with the halo of regret as the parting scene beside the ship that gave me passage to the sunny isle that now fosters the remembrance of the lengthened-out struggles of Theodore Parker. When I recall my death-bed scene, and mingle its waters with the tide of grief that assailed me at Boston Harbor, I can not compare those graphic pictures, delineated on the tablet of memory, with any preponderance of affection shown or tears dropped at my departure. Boston claims my energetic investment of strength; claims my manhood-endeavors to foster the seeds of love and harmony, and carry my weapon of courage to battle the iron door of oppression that is swinging on its hinges for the release of human weakness, and emancipation from the errors of the past.

CHAPTER XVII.

ONE more word, and then I will pick up my spirit-staff, and point the way my footsteps are now tending. Earth holds her banner of strength in accumulated deeds. The tinsel and glitter of false pretense have no weight in the great scales of human happiness. All individuality must touch a vibrating cord in the under-current of human greatness. All mankind seek a culminating point of honor, seek the glory achieved in imaginative moments of worth to the soul. Earth is one vast play-ground, and all seeking to touch the goal of public acceptance. Every play has its reference of approval fixed in the minor scales of the world's judgment. Earth holds her banner of trust for all time: she has her despairing moments, and sees no end to the besetting curse of sin. But the illuminated points of God's beneficent purposes shine in on the troubled waters of Old Earth's career; and she folds again her hands with the full assurance that her rudder of strength is in the grasp of a propelling force anterior, and above her power of ability to control. When the majesty of this theme sweeps across the magnetic fibers of my soul, I feel the inspiration from the dissolving truths wafted through ten thousand channels, and speaking in their ever-varying tongues of hope, peace, and joy over the fruitions of earth. Mankind has only commenced drinking at the fountain of life. The waters that quench their thirst to-day are but a drop beside the majestic stream that will irrigate the ice-bound shores of Time. The deluge that shall next sweep the world will be a flood of truth; and no ark of safety will need to ride its waters, and no dove will be sent forth to proclaim the subsiding of the elements of peace that will follow in the wake of truth. The altar-fires of heaven are glowing with revelations to be given to the world as fast as the hand of Science clears away the rubbish that has so long presided over the affairs of men. The auxiliary steps to be taken to clear the channels leading to the mythical heaven of all superstition, of all allegorical matter, of all the presumption of creeds, and of all false precepts and examples that darken the doorway of faith, and leave us strugglers around a truth we can not fathom, are these ; let Charity preside over the world's board of error ; let Love dip her wings in all the stagnant waters beside the stream of life, and let Wisdom lead the way to a correct understanding of the great central sun of our ultimate destiny ; and so let mankind journey, with the true knowledge, not born of hope, but in the science of God's word : and light will spring up in all dark places, and no stumbling-blocks will appear on the roadway of life.

THE END OF THE FIRST CANTO.

CHAPTER XVIII.

It may seem strange for me to state my present ability to preside over the affairs of mankind on earth ; but the statement is nevertheless correct, and I am impressed with the duty to explain spirit-elevation above the crude affinity of earth. This disclosure will test the utmost powers of comprehension, and still I will give it in as clear and lucid a manner as words can express the thoughts I shall utter. Spirit-communion has ever been an established fact ; and, although mankind have preached and prayed from that fountain of living worth, it has, until recent years, been clothed in mystery, and talked about as a world we could not fathom, as a world

of awe not soluble by any code of faith, or any power of
comprehension that mind had attained to, until the gen-
tle and low-toned raps were heard at Rochester, and
those silvery chimes, so fraught with hope and strength
to the world, startled the nineteenth century, and awakened them to a sense of putting on a cap of thought,
and sending out the spirit of investigation to fathom the
significance of those unseen sounds. The world at large
dropped the brand of " humbug " on those tiny efforts of
spirit-control. The world has ever cried " humbug ! "
to a theory not understood, has ever assailed a truth with
weapons of defense, and sought no advantage over the
errors of the past ; but the wheel of Time has dropped
truths for mankind to sift, regardless of any hue and cry
of public favor. Will mankind please to remember that
every advance step over ignorant assumption has dug its
way through the fiery furnace of discordant elements,
seared, scorched, and blasted by the infernal machinery
of human laws ; but Truth ever seats herself with a triumphant smile, high and dry above any code of human
enactment to frustrate or dishonor. Spirit-communion
is the bar let down for the world's redemption and restoration from the sin of Adam's fall ; spirit-communion is
the harbinger of the coming man that is to lead the way
to life everlasting, and flood the world with a new baptism and a new birth. Then will the glory of the Lamb
appear in a cloud of truth over benighted Christianity,
and the veil of mysticism and doubt will no longer hang
over the world. I took my departure from earth, or, rather,
from my material body, with the full assurance of reten-
tive individuality. Up to the last moment of earth's mas-
tery, I possessed my power of thought distinct, possessed

the power to trace myself through space, possessed the faculty to feel myself in space; my physical body was losing its charm, days before my spirit took its flight; my bed of sickness was radiant with hope; and I had the drifting halo of peace beside me daily. When, at the last hour of my stay with mortality, the death-film shut friends and attendants from my outward vision, my spirit took in the full and complete detail of the dying scene; and, were I an artist, I could sketch it to the life, for it hangs in my gallery of memory fadeless, and dewy with the inspiration of loving friendship: I hold that scene in sacred keeping. I can not lift the spell that attaches me to earth, because the sympathetic cord is galvanized with the true essence of salvation; that is, the dew of the harmonial law pervading all space: therefore, when I seek earth, I clothe myself with the ether dew of my habitation, and seek the corresponding element in humanity. I seek the cord of sympathy, or sympathetic emotion: that law runs parallel with the law of cause and effect. It may be well for me to explain the sympathetic law, or the binding law that runs through all materiality and through all spirituality: it is the force and coercive law that moves the machinery of Nature; it is the cause of things made, and it begets its own formation. Like begets like in every code of order. The formation of worlds is accomplished by the sympathetic movement of elementary matter. The cohesive strata in earth attach the primates to a focus of strength; and repeated effort at centralization causes a rounded-out form of matter. Let me give an illustration; take, for instance, a globule or drop of water; condense that by freezing; it may assume a variety of shapes: but let a sympathetic sunstroke touch those particles of congealed water, and they instantly assume the rounded-out form of mother-earth, showing conclusively that the primates in matter strictly adhere to first principles. Dissolve particles of earth, for instance; you will find that the minutest portion is in keeping with the great mass from which it was removed. This is a complex study, the law of centralization, the law that sticks to first principles. You can not destroy one particle of earth, you can not fix it or shape it, but what its ultimate will assume its mother-form; and that same law runs through all substance. The formation system has its birth from a necessity in the financiering of elementary motion. The first driftings of earth's commotion were crude efforts, not legalized in history, for the very reason that speech was denied our first parents. That effort in man was accomplished by elongated power over respiratory motion. Man in his first development was only removed from the beast by intuitive reason, therefore, made capable of improvement, susceptible to external influences, holding a key of strength to unlock the cycles of time, and round out to the full estate of a world in motion. Man is but a counterpart of Nature: every element in the storehouse of earth finds its sympathetic monitor in man's outward construction; and the radiating influences in man dip their beaks in the worlds that motionary earth has etherealized, and sent into space. That thought is glowing with grandeur, and finds sympathetic accordance in the world I now inhabit. Man radiates to his true purpose through the same law that particles of earth assume a standard shape; but for the law of sympathy

the world would be motionless, congealed into frozen
antipathy, with no sunbeams to illuminate her secret
springs of action ; and, but for the law of sympathy in
the binding forces of intellectuality, there would be no
stamp-mark to insure the meed of approval.

CHAPTER XIX.

THEREFORE, as I before stated, when I seek earth, I
clothe myself with the conditions of earth, — clothe myself in a condition to reach that atmosphere. It is merely
a similitude of the changes that are necessary on earth
to meet the changes in atmospheric pressure ; or it is
simply a change of clothing to suit the locality we are
journeying to. What satisfies the body in summer
time is in no way suitable for a winter's atmosphere ;
and when Earth fails in her atmospheric conditions to
supply the part of man that belongs to her, then the
higher law steps in to the rescue, and folds an arm of
strength and sympathy around the spiritual element ; or
that condition in man that needs a change of climate.
Man possesses the element of change in exact ratio with
the changes in Earth. We see the Earth with our vision
of Earth ; but we can not with that Earth-vision see her
secret springs of motion. Are we, then, to doubt the existence of her ethereal life, — her life of silvery harmony,
that throws off her crude material, and goes on with her
work of reproduction, but always with reference to the
higher law ; always changing her material, throwing off

the old, and putting on the new; always clothing her spirit with new beauty and symmetry of design ? Earth has her spiral forces that point heavenward. She holds within her receptacles the monitors that grasp the unseen cords of sympathy that keep green her fields, and ripen her vineyards of strength, to still further the law of sympathy existing between her outward surface and the component parts of man's organic structure. You can not separate man from earth, because the law of sympathy outlasts time. There will ever be an element in man that will correspond with the intuition in Nature. Nature can not tell why she builds. It is not because she has not the power of expression; for her face proclaims her power of speech in ten thousand low and mellow sounds, and speaks in every variety of dialect that human nature can fathom. Still she refuses to utter the whys and wherefores of her existence; but I ween, at some future day, there will be a revelation from Old Nature that will fix her starting-point, and show the consistency of mind in matter.

CHAPTER XX.

The intuitive faculties in Nature correspond precisely with the intuitive law in man and animal. It is simply the capacity to draw productive power when needed, — simply the power to collect re-enforcements by the internal element of demand. Man, animal, and Nature reach out the aspiring hand of want to the spiral fountain of life, whose springs we can not see with Nature's vision, but whose wealth we may feel in every strata of mind and matter. Heaven has fixed her stamp-mark on every particle of earth's fruition : she holds her claim serene and majestic, with no ripples of doubt to mar her quiet surface of content. Heaven and earth are partners for life. You can not divorce their system of operation ; it is co-existent with the deity of purpose, twin in sympathetic emotion and vibratory accordance : and that they are nearing in their ultimate destiny is evident from the non-satisfaction evinced in bygone theories. Man is sure to bring heaven and earth together, because man holds the power to act from reason : all other vibratory activity is consequent on the law of cause and effect, or the law of give and take. Man is the focus of strength uniting the two worlds, sure to elevate the earth by taxation on heaven, if need be ; and as that is the last demand made for the benefit of humanity, it is evident that the past promulgation of theological bombast is losing its power of control, and humanity are seeking those fields of living green, whose fadeless worth will frustrate every ill that sorrowing Earth takes to her platform of use.

CHAPTER XXI.

My present locality, to use a symbolized expression, is a gem found beside the river of the stream of life. It is the pearl expressive of great future worth. I have arrived, by constant application, to the third constellation of shining luster, — the third realm inhabitable in space. It is located in proximate affinity to Taurus or the Pleiades, that nebula of stars situated in the constellation of Andromeda. The atmosphere of my present locality is fragrant with the dew of hope : I am clothed in the vestments of a June morning on earth ; or, rather, I am clad in the white garments of peace. Clothing, in the spirit-world, is emblematical of the conditions of the soul. White signifies peace, a chastened condition gained from culture in every stage of development. My abode lacks nothing to my present growth ; every niche is filled with satisfaction to my soul. Those on the earth-plane who conjecture the soul to be mythical — a fleeting, shadowy, ethereal something, not tangible by faith or actual demonstration — will no doubt be surprised and incredulous when I here declare the soul to be a substantial, living embodiment of growth and consequent power. The soul is the essence of manhood or of childhood ; it is the intellectual tissues woven into symmetry of motion, — the thinking apparatus distinct in operation, bearing similitude to its casket of clay. The man of earth-proportions is the husk that protects the kernel through the earth-experience, no more needed when the kernel is ready for the harvesting. Earth takes care of her part with ready skill and consummate art, that hides her secret springs of action. Man was never known to search in earth for any thing belonging to himself: his intuitive reason points above the materialistic plane of life. What is there in Nature that satisfies man above the wants that Nature manifests? Man ever has a star of hope in the ascendant, ever an illuminated pathway leading from the grave, ever a pillar of strength in history, or some by-path of his own finding ; then wherefore is it, when we in spirit-life seek to make conjecture a living reality, seek to personify spirit-life, seek the divine afflatus of strength to carry our work on earth, that the opposing elements meet us with their pointed daggers of distrust, and a hang-dog look of shame at being found in the field of investigation for facts to corroborate the sly inklings of truth so often dogged at, but seldom hit.

CHAPTER XXII.

I will again resume my point of local bearing to the world, and test the credulity of my fellow-beings on earth. I before said, that white was emblematical of peace. My vestments are real to the sphere I inhabit. This ethereality, or spirit-costume, was taken on at what is termed the death-hour. Let me here explain the procedure of spirit-ability to assume the ethereal costume that the vision of earth can not detect. Let us assume that spirit is the breath breathed into man at birth. Can we, with our earth-vision, see that breath ? see the power that ushers life into a structure formed through Nature's laws ? Are we, then, to doubt that power, that unseen capacity in man, that vibrates to the myriads of keys in Nature's wardrobe of use ? If man is to doubt every thing not in keeping with his earth-vision, then may he doubt his earth-existence because he can not see his power of life. His locomotive springs of action are hid from the outward view. It is only the interior, the spirit, that feels the life-springs of motion; feels the electric current permeating all space; feels the power to soar above the outward form; and, possessing that power, it necessarily reveals itself. Therefore, when I say the soul walks away from its clothing of earth, I state a fact that is soluble to reason.

CHAPTER XXIII.

WERE mankind to allow reason a freer scope, it would impart new vigor to the life-forces of action. Man has yet to learn that reason is the key that unlocks the scientific world, and brings the treasure of life to a basis of truth where no doubt can disturb its sure foundation. My ethereal life is clothed with vestments of substantial evidence to the society that occupy my sphere in the order of progression. The fabric in which we clothe ourselves is tangible to our sense of touch; and, when I say it is all woven in the looms of earth, I state another fact that I must prove with the key of reason. The fabric, or illusory material, as earth terms spirit-clothing, is the *finesse*, or the art in Nature, of the outwrought materials of earth. It is the fancy dictum of the interior design; it is the test-mark of inorganic substance, the nerve-portion underlying the outspoken design. Let me illustrate. In order to bring out a design, whether in substance to clothe a material body, or in the conception of some grander scheme, reared for the world's benefit, it is necessary to fashion the fabric or structure on the internal plane of thought; and the mind that fashions on earth takes that same power of design to the higher sphere of use. The condition of the soul always seeks its affinity in artistic worth and ability. Therefore, when I say spirit-vestments are a condition of the soul, it is no more than saying that my earth-garments were the outwrought fancy or condition of my mind or soul. My fancy, when on earth, led me to the attire of black; and now, when I near earth, I assume the old condition of mind. And those that see with the light of clairvoyance always see me in my suit of black. Let me give another illustration. Take, for instance, the color of green. Now, the combination of oxidized gases compose the prismatic shades in that one color. Note, for instance, the shading of a rainbow. Does it ever occur to the public mind that man, on earth, helps to fashion the rainbow? Let me explain the process by which it is done. Rainbows assume the different shades of coloring. Sometimes we see them span the heavens dressed in the rosy tints of morning; at other times, they don their blue-tinted robes; and ofttimes they appear in the shimmering dress of green, showing, conclusively, that the system of change is not confined to earth; and also showing the disposition in ethereal space to harmonize and blend the true elements of purpose in constructing the rainbow. As I before remarked, man on earth helps to fashion the rainbow through the law of give and take. Man on earth possesses the power, through chemical process, to embody the electric currents or the prismatic shades that vibrate through the universe of color. Now, as man possesses the ability to embody the primates, or bring out a color from pri-

5

mordial confusion, he possesses the power to embody that color in space; and there it undergoes the process of blending. Those on earth who suppose that labor ceases at the expiration of material existence, will be surprised to know that the truth of labor is accomplished in the spirit-world, that the essence, or ideal, finds shape through the active energies of spirit-life. Color is a condition of the soul. I have my earth-conditioned garments, my spiral-pointed armor, which bears the rosy hue of morning; and my white robe of peace, that assimilates with my present condition of mind. I might here state that life is a condition of soul, — the only condition that remains firm to its trust, because life is soul, the intuitive essence that symbolizes structure, and manifests itself in outwrought design.

CHAPTER XXIV.

I WILL now take up my present condition in space: and, to the eye of faith, I am doing the Lord's will; but in reality I am on the direct road of progressive movement, having followed out the dictates of conscience, my monitor of strength, in ushering me along the road of salvation, until this present time finds me in a condition to master every difficulty that impeded my progress on earth. My condition of soul is in harmony with the system of laws through which I labor. I am in no way constrained. Labor assumes its standard worth: each department has its pointer of use, directing me onward and upward to pick in fields not yet open to earth. My road lies up the steep and rugged hill of duty. I claim no wings of flight aside from those tipped with the ether dew of use.

CHAPTER XXV.

I AM at this present time folding the leaves of my past biography. It is written on the fine tissued sheets of vellum manufactured from etherealized substance found in the second sphere : it is a species of galvanized rubber-lasting prepared from oxidized gases or fluids ; it is done through chemical process, brought to a higher focus of power than earth claims at present. Galvanized rubber forms a part of the basis of etherealized atmosphere : it is the soluble part to the outward sense. The other portions of ether forming the electric currents in atmospheric conditions have their basis in the minutiæ of earth soluble to that code of reason that acknowledges the ether dew or the *finesse dictum* in all substance, — the portions of earth that throw off the strata or inorganic particles that compose space ; the portion that contains the sympathetic monitor, or the portion that graduates to intelligence. That may be a new thought to some, that matter contains any intellectual parts ; but there is a strata running through all matter possessing the component element of intellectuality. It was that same element in mother-earth that made man upright, and endowed with reason. Mother-earth has ceased to build from the bygone fashion, because the necessity is passed; and the higher law came to the rescue as soon as reason could exert a sway outside of primordial substance. Then Nature had accomplished her highest effort, and man then possessed a key to unlock old Nature, and bring her to the platform of investigation, to find her subtle element or elements that compose the spiral points of reason. In a work that the ensuing spring will bring before the public, the Alpha and Omega of spirit-claim on and over the rudimental shaping of earth will be tested. The work I here advertise will embrace the primordial confusion of matter, and bring out the strata of mind that wrought structure and shape from confused inharmony of chaotic ruin.

CHAPTER XXVI.

My present condition of life is rather picturesque: I have my harbor of refuge, my home of secret pleasure and thought, my fancy-wrought Castle of Ease in the ascending scale of progress. I think every person has a local habitation of ease somewhere in the future; and that breastwork, thrown up for the soul to reach and mount, keeps green the field of hope, and leads us out to span the unseen shores of time and eternity. My present home winds its sustaining arm of strength around my every wish and purpose. I find gifts for the soul in every corner of my local habitation. Let me here describe my seat of honor, or, in other words, give the exact dimensions of my spirit-home. As I before stated, my local resort is situated in the third sphere, near the constellation of Andromeda : it bears the tropical clime along its smooth and undulating plots of verdured green. My mansion of rest from active duty is in the suburban style, with broad parterre and sylvan haunts that vibrate to the mystic touches of my white-robed angel friends. But to make my home more definite, more tangible to earth, I will give it in the form of a parable ; I will dress it up in allegory, but with the stamp-mark of truth facing every side of my spirit-edifice. We term spirit the life, the pulp of being, the interior casket, that takes precedence in going a journey, or going to rest, or in any effort that requires movement. The spirit first starts the team of strength that moves the outward edifice. Let us, then, suppose the interior portion of man, the casket of strength, the pulp of being, desires to outstrip time ; desires to build from the interior plane of thought ; that is, desires to fashion a structure that time can not control. The very desire is outwrought on the spirit-camera in space ; the desire is the structure. You desire to build a material edifice ; that is, you desire the protection of the material body, and your mind fashions from material substance : but, in every particle of material substance, there is spirit-architecture, there is life wrought out in what seems dead structure. Now, the homes upreared from thought and application on the earth-plane are daguerreotyped on soluble atmosphere, before the earth-provision is made. We speak of weaving our castles of fancy when those fancy-wrought castles are the real structures of endurance that Time apes at, but only reaches in a bungling manner. We can not build on the earth-basis as finely as spirit can conjecture ; and why is

that nonconformity to thought apparent in every symbolized edifice on the footstool of Time, if thought found
in matter its fruition of purpose ?

CHAPTER XXVII.

My spirit-home is an establishment of unpretending
merit as far as its local purposes are concerned, or as far
as it supplies the attachments that the past can claim.
It serves as my restaurant of growth at present, or my
refuge from impending storms that threaten every cargo
of strength on the boundless sea of Time.   Let me here
state that eternity is Time, an outreach from the system
of days, weeks, months, and years ; but still it is Time on
the wing.   A higher schedule of purpose, a loftier tone
of thought, propelled by the steam-car of progress.   My
spirit-home has a foundation-site that borders on the
stream of Life ; it fronts the chapel of Duty, and has a
corner hedge of Doubt to dispel the inglowing ease of
conditional circumstances.   My home is adorned with
pictures of art ; the walls are frescoed with the true art
in Nature.   I have my study-room, my system of study,
or my system of thought, brought to actual use ; I have
my reception-room, where I meet my spirit-friends in social converse, where we gather strings of pearls, and
count them for the benefit of each other.   My friend
Rufus Choate proposed to me at one of our usual
gatherings the utility of constructing a system where
the electric band can be used, and spirits *en rapport* with

mortals etherealize the electric current passing round the band, and thereby assimilate space to the understanding of the medium operator : that would be.worthy of investigation on earth ; and the construction of the band will test spirit-ability to personify themselves on independent conditions. A word to the wise may be productive of beneficial results, and the harbinger of the opening day when the glory of the heavens will appear, not in the burning bush, but in the mellowed tints of pearl-freighted paradise.

CHAPTER XXVIII.

In constructing the band for spirit-messages or spirit-personations, it will require some skill in management. The band should be made of perforated isinglass ; the punctures should be very fine, and made equidistant from each other. The ones operating in spirit-realms have a basis of rubber, that being more easily procured ; but, for earth-purposes, the isinglass would be more preferable, because atmospheric conditions would have less effect, and isinglass could be brought to a finer state of consistency. Let the band be made from one to two inches in width ; let the perforations be accomplished with a very fine pointed instrument. This band can be worn on any portion of the body, only graduate the size. Isinglass can be brought to a state of elasticity by the chemical process of blending oxylized gases, or the nitrate of silver in harmonious parts with the fundaments of glutinous substance. The band can be made with very little expense, and would be very beneficial in detecting spirit-power. Spirits can only work under conditional circumstances, as man on the earth-sphere has to deal with the conditions requisite to the purpose he serves; and let me here state, that conditional spiritualism must take root before the true element will flourish. Mankind, in seeking spirit-communion, should first seek the conditions whereby spirits can come *en rapport* with mortals. If man on earth seeks a change of destiny or circumstances, seeks a change in his local bearing to the world, every condition requisite for the change is observed; but, when man comes to spirit-conditions in spirit-manifestations, he seems to ignore every system or combination-force in their mode of communication. How is it that man drinks in so little sense when diving for the pearl of great price that has so long been in deep water ?

CHAPTER XXIX.

LET me now take up my occupation, and bear my burdens back to the world, to be there tested and weighed in the balance with common sense and justice of acknowledgment. The majority of people on the earth-plane of existence suppose that spirit-life is divested of all care and labor, that we float in space, or have seats of honor surrounding the throne of God, where praise and thanksgiving is the continual theme of evangelical life. Now, those who accept that life of ease and worship will look upon my life as being too practical for heaven; but those who knew me on the earth-principle of life would fully understand my incapacity for serving dead-letters. That may seem impious; but, to a reflective mind, God's throne of worship is the universe of deeds, and God's realms of space are glowing with the active energies of disembodied mortals. All labor must have a systematized footing; must have aqueducts of use leading from that system, and pillars of strength to sustain the embryotic principle of worth that maintains its position above any altar of pride, or distilled flummery that mankind manufactured from the idle driftings of polished fastidiousness and corrupt inglory of content.

CHAPTER XXX.

My spirit-home has never frustrated one desire of my earth-ability to perform my duty of purpose in maintaining my system of thought toward the high and holy calling of promulgating the true seeds of the Christian religion. My spirit-life takes form in active works: I see my way through active precision of movement. A friend of mine called at my study a short time since for the purpose of investigating the by-ways of poverty in the Second Ward of Progress. My friend stated the condition of one district or locality where God's pruning-hook of knowledge had scarcely found an entrance. The inhabitants of that locality are steeped in famine and want: they are the offshoots from the lower grades of social life on earth. And let me here state, that heaven's door is open to all life ; but the platform has a signal-gun that fires a bullet of disapproval at every intruder that shows a lack of the current material surrounding the gates of Paradise.

CHAPTER XXXI.

I HAVE many ways for the exercise of energetic effort. I have a school where the sciences are expounded ; where we bring earth up for proofs in her keeping that will expand our altars of thought, and cause earth to appear like the background in some fairy-scene. Earth holds her pent-up treasures with the grasp of despair. The fore-wind of knowledge is sweeping her fettered fields, and laying waste the props that sustain her dynasties of ignorant power. Earth has never yet laid open her secret caverns for the world's investigation. The law of ignorance has bound her selfish chains until the stroke from the fire-altars of heaven proclaimed the victory over benighted Christendom. My soul cries out for light, for gifts outside of the impending stroke of pen. I would fain call down God's truths from wells overflowing with love, light, and knowledge ; from worlds that span the broad arena above my platform of comparative growth. But the World must be handled with gloved fingers : it will not do to hasten her development. The ploughshare of Truth cuts deep and wide, and also bears a leveler in front to beat aside the corrupt cumbrances of Time.

CHAPTER XXXII.

My spirit-life bears unction of grandeur and power in thought and purpose to serve mankind as long as services from my sphere of gleanings are required or needed. I am laboring now to establish free moral government, independent of sex, color, hierarchy, or monarchy; independent of creed, statue, or the press. That may seem a broad sweep for freedom; but it is, nevertheless, the true aim of freedom. Individualization is sure to be accomplished. Each mind must become a world unto itself; and every star that sets in the ascendent throws out a focus of light that illuminates the channels of earth. My duty lies in the direction of all fettered institutions of reform; and, while I seek to dispel evil in spirit-life, I seek an open portal to reach earth, and lay my flag of truce beside the quartered enemy of doubt and fear. I have the glowing thought of use ever beside my wandering footsteps, ever prompting me to search and find for the storehouse of memory and for the storehouse of humanity. You can not separate the element of purpose existing between memory and humanity: they are co-existing in friendship, parallel in purpose to serve each other, and deft in the use of instruments propelling their movements. Memory holds her shield of thought high and dry above the conditions of time, and bears her eminent seat back to earth by the overland route, and seeks no other way, only the one left open by cause and effect.

CHAPTER XXXIII.

SPIRIT-LIFE has too long hung a dead-weight on the shoulders of Time. The incubus of ease and quiet that has so long surrounded the throne eternal is preparing graduated seats, and for ever closing the passage to that long leap in the dark that has for ages hung a pall of terror around the destiny of man. Wherefore has this change been wrought? and wherefore are mankind seeking the element of purpose in their outreach after heaven? Is it not because God's favored few fail to procure a hearing at the seat of reason? and is it not because mythology sickens the soul, and dampens the energies of faith and hope? The nineteenth century is seeking a new heaven and a new earth. The spirit of energetic movement feels cramped and dwarfed in purpose in the confined atmosphere of sectarian by-paths and lodgments for the soul's ease and immolated daring. The spirit of unrest is traveling the earth, seeking the items that the hand of Fate drops in the car of Time; and the spirit of unrest is ushering in the New Jerusalem; is picking up the staff of common sense, and traveling out on the progressive road that leads to ultimate success, and also leads to ultimate happiness by the diverging lines drawn by active duty in every vineyard on the course of time.

CHAPTER XXXIV.

LET me here say, that my present occupation is just as real, just as much an embodied fact, just as much an effort to carry out a purpose, to culminate a design formed by the will, as was any effort I ever made on earth to further a scheme fostered by my reason. There is no such thing as an illusion: every shadow has its substance; and every inlaid principle its embodiment in art. Spirit is the reality of a personated being, the life-giving element to design, the spiral point that reaches above matter, the focus of power on earth, and the ultimate of man. Spiritualization is the heaven of earth, the *finale* of all matter. The world will never know where it left its material body, never realize the utter baptism of dogmatic prejudice. The world is nearing a great social earthquake: there will not be so much as a pillar left of the old formula and systematic worship, and by-plays of social epologue, that furnishes a whip and driver, but no fitting harness, to travel the road of life in. Society must outgrow its stern decree of rule, its system of slavery, that furnishes a beaten track that individual effort must walk in. I ignore the force of rule; I ignore any system that carries the lash of coercion, and the hoodwink of public deception to the world's arena of strength. I may not give another combined experience to the world. This work has occupied my leisure moments since the 24th of July last; and, in giving it to the public, I have labored under great disadvantages: but I would have it fully and distinctly understood, that I have carried the point for which I labored. Let me touch one more point of spirit-duty, give one more galvanic shock to the world; and then I will prepare for publication the work I have before alluded to, entitled "Marigolds by the Wayside." It will be the prose and poetry of life, the actual and ideal, which is the áctual imperfectly understood.

CHAPTER XXXV.

AN APPENDIX TO THE FOREGOING WORK.

In giving an appendix to this work, it will be necessary to state my object in so doing. Human nature is prone to doubting; prone to see what is not, in preference to what is. I can not divest myself of the idea that 1869 will leave the world flooded with more truth and knowledge than any previous year in the calendar of Time. The reason of my adding an appendix to a work already completed is the faith I have in words coupled with works; and I never yet finished a subject of thought, but what more could have been said to advantage. That may seem egotistical; but egotism, to a certain extent, is necessary. It would be unwise to ignore the true art of thinking. The true purpose of thought serves in the world. Thought is the essence of a purpose, the aroma that floats around a design; thought is the distilling dew to meditation, the secret spring that puts the machinery of the world in motion.

Therefore, when thought seeks to gather for the service of mankind, let the seeds of appreciation sometimes drop by the wayside.

CHAPTER XXXVI.

IN fitting out a ship to cross the ocean, great care is observed in having every part serve the purpose for which it is designed; and so, when man starts out on the voyage of life, it is well to have his sails set in the right direction; to have his ship of thought bear anchor at every port where science and philosophy have dropped a cargo to be lifted on board for the world's strength and honor. Mankind, as a general principle, lack in the system of thought; lack the power of application to delve out a structure whose basis is an inlaid principle of mind. The power of mind is, to a great extent, fashioned from necessity. Man never attains to his full hight when cradled in the lap of luxury. It is the stern winter of adverse circumstances, the stern decree of Fate weaving its web of cunning meshes with the intricate finger of Content, to be thrown around the first bidder for honors in the kingdom of heaven. Thought fashions from a necessity in the motionary elements of Time. There is no expansion to thought unless excited from the outside world; unless the reins of government be thrown at the organ of visual sense, and caught at by the finger of Want: and then Thought steps down from her pedestal of ease, and manufactures skill from the conception of use. Thought is only indolent from non-ability of physical movement; whether it be insufficiency in organized parts or the inactivity of muscular effort, both have the neutralizing effect on the viscera of sense. Indolence is the moth that eats away the time-table of man, and leaves him floating in space, aimless, purposeless, and almost soulless; a drug to be fostered by the energetic law of recompense. Man on earth is fool-hardy and unwise to tamper with time, to let his well-springs of thought dry up and choke to death for the want of a balance-wheel in the outside world to light up the springs of action to furnish the evidences that he has lived, and lived to a purpose in life.

CHAPTER XXXVII.

THE Carthagenian War spread its devastating influence around the whole Romish empire: the feudal force of arms swept the Roman Senate clear of the pillared wrongs, that, year after year, had convened at the citadel of strength. War ever holds a purifying tone in the background; ever lights the future with a torch of hope, and feels the victory won as a new start on the road of principle. The true essence of war is purification; and the next-signal gun will be fired at the national treasury-house of Sin. The Future of earth will burnish her board of deal with a lithographic design, where principles will rear an honest background, and the children of earth can be seen reflected with new aims to fashion their career in life. The tidal wave of Time moves the great ocean of man's eventful career; era after era sweeps along the uneven track of the world's destiny. The harbinger of peace ever walks in the ascending pathway; the glory of the rising generation will be wafted on high by the trumpeters of truth that will be set over the lost tribes of Israel.

CHAPTER XXXVIII.

THE world is nearing the great blending crisis when Jew and Gentile will drink of the wine prepared as a ritual of saving ordinance, and a breastplate of church desecration. It is time that the blood of Christ be served from the standpoint of principle, instead of the upheaved holocaust of sacrificial altars and synods of heterodox mummery. The Christian era is laboring out of her toils; is bending the bow of promise to every rational mind, and lifting the salvation-seat above the shoes of men. The Christian era was born of a principle; the outwrought structure of Christ mingled its healing influence with the old Jewish assumption of power and idolatrous worship. Christ's first presentation was from a humble standpoint of view. He was the meek and loving Saviour, the one with God in spirit, the one clothed with immortality for the whole race of mankind; but successive years have changed the whole outward bearing of Christ's mission on earth. Who thinks of worshiping Christ in sackcloth and ashes at the present

time? Who, of all that are seated along the broad-aisles
of the world's fashionable churches drink in the true
spirit of the Christian Godhead? Christ is the adorning
grace in every sanctification-seat reared for the world's
benefit; but it is the outward emblem that precedes the
inglowing beauty of the loving Jesus. It is plain to be
seen that Christ's spirit of meekness is not the dress
worn on the all-important once a week, when the true
spirit of the Christian religion is dwarfed, and worn like
a plaster of penance, to be removed when the " Amen "
drops from the pillared sanctuary: it is plain to be seen
that Christ is dressed in effigy; that his adorning grace
is an outside covering, worn for the benefit of public
opinion. When Christ becomes the standard-bearer of
principles instead of the background to a system of
slavery, and the holly-branch to wave for the world's
pride and egotistical bearing, then will Gethsemane
sprout the true basis of the Christian era.

CHAPTER XXXIX.

My next work will contemplate the duties of the
Christian religion; show the true meaning of Christ,
or, in other words, the prose and poetry of his career.
It will be delving some ways for first principles; but, in
order to have a solid foundation, there must be an under-
current from which to fashion the living stream. There
is nothing so conducive to happiness as a firm trust on
an unperverted God. Nothing so expands the mind as

searching for the imperishable seed from which our lives took root. The God of Abraham, Isaac, and Jacob, still flourishes the wand of peace around the world's board of salvation. The God of Israel speaks in all the modern dialects, and in all modern institutions of reform, and in the whispering winds that proclaim the shattered glory of the olden anarchy of wrongs. Future years will rear a Godhead or Principality of Power that will flourish like the green bay-tree, and throw out a branch of hope to every soul on the highway for the principle of life. Justice demands a change in the Godhead; and the law of equity and right are clamorous to establish the principle of Infinite Power beyond the reach of a personal God to demolish. The tread-wheel of Time will lay an evacuation-fee on all the incidental whipping-posts and scourging-rods that ignorance has reared by the wayside. God will yet speak to the understanding of mankind. He will yet rear a foundation-seat in the world that the mind can grasp, and see the safety-valve through which the world will pass to its regeneration-seat.

CHAPTER XL.

I MUST give this work to the world from my stand-point of spiritual growth; and, from a spiritual stand-point, I must dedicate the element of reform. I would have the Alpha and Omega of spiritualism an abiding emblem of contentment and peace. I would have the Rock of Ages cleft to the center, and fashioned to the understanding of mankind ; I would have the beauty of Christ's life worn as an every-day suit by the world's nationality ; I would have Christ triumph in a world he came to save, and in a world that has so long lighted its taper of knowledge at his fountain-head ; I would have Christ the recognized element along the road of progress ; and, finally, I would have Christ the redeeming quality in mankind, the star whose splendor is to reflect the kingdom of heaven on earth.

THE END.